Selling Uncorked

Increase Sales Through Party Etiquette

Ward Figge

Edited by
Caleb Jeiel Figge

This publication is designed to provide
accurate and authoritative information
concerning the subject matter covered. Its
intentions are not to render legal, accounting or
other professional services. If professional
services are desired, contact the services of a
competent professional.

ISBN: 1440422435
EAN-13: 9781440422430

Dedicated to my three wonderful children:

Cassidy Nakita Figge

Caleb Jeiel Figge

Ciera Nicole Figge

Contents

Contents (continued)

Acknowledgements

No one writes a book without many people helping. This book is no exception.

I would like to thank my family, friends and co-workers who encouraged me to put my concepts and ideas on paper.

There are too many people to name, but to all my acquaintances, friends and loved ones, please know how thankful I am.

A few people are too humble to be mentioned, but they spent countless hours challenging me to re-think my approach. These people (and you know who you are), were instrumental in the completion of this book.

Forward

Salespeople love to go to parties. Why? Because they love people and relationships. Selling is the greatest party ever. *Selling Uncorked* shows you how to treat selling like a party and have the time of your life. Sales and parties have many similarities that you will discover as you read this book. Most people already know proper etiquette for attending a party, but seem apprehensive when it comes to selling. It does not have to be that way. Every party is different just like every sales presentation is different. If you are prepared and know the proper skills for interacting with others, you will be the talk of your company.

When I first got involved with public speaking, a pastor told me that it is very simple to speak in front of others. He told me if you know the proper way to create and follow an outline you will give an effective speech. In the same way, this book is your outline to career advancement and the pleasure of what is considered one of the greatest professions on earth, which is selling.

The information and tips you glean from this book will put your mind at ease from the stress of "selling" prospects, as you learn to apply party principles to your sales calls. Your prospects will go from "being sold" to wanting to do business with you.

Enjoy!

Introduction

This book will help you be focused on selling and draw from your own experiences at parties to uncork your sales. You get to decide what "uncorked" means to you. It could mean more money. It could mean more satisfaction. It could mean more passion about your career. Whatever it is that you desire the principles in this book will help you get there.

I believe selling can be boiled down to the following phrase. Salespeople *"visit old friends and make new friends."* This "meeting" of friends is exactly what you do at a party and that is why parties are a great analogy for the sales process.

All art (including the written word) is the revelation of one's self. Good art draws on the things all people have in common, and in doing so, translates into useful information for the recipient or observer. As you learn new sales concepts and draw on your own experiences, especially good parties you have attended, this information will pop off the page into your daily sales life. You get to paint the picture of your life. The concepts found on the following pages will add some color to your artwork.

The thought of attending a party is exciting. It is my hope that your sales career will become just as exciting.

Selling Uncorked

Chapter One

Where's the Party

Do you remember high school? If your memory is foggy, let me help. For many of you, the most important thing in your life was finding the rockin' party being thrown that week. This usually came down to whose parents were out of town or whose parents were cool enough to let you throw a party. It may be a long time since high school, but when it comes to loving parties, nothing has changed. People still love to party and selling is very similar to going to a party.

The question for you is - Are any of your prospects throwing a party soon? By party, I mean are there any opportunities to make a sales presentation?

We all enter the business world with varying people skills and when it comes to dealing with people, it takes many types of personalities for a company to be successful. In sales, introverts can be as successful as extroverts can. Why is this the case? Prospects vary in their own personalities and therefore have certain types of personalities they prefer to buy from and do business with. It is human nature to feel comfortable around certain types of people. It is important to understand the human side of selling. The best way to understand this is to observe different personality types at a party.

What does it take to be a successful salesperson?

Successful salespeople have three arrows in their sales quiver - to use a hunting analogy. They have the sales trinity, which includes *trust, charisma* and *product knowledge*. All three are necessary, but not all three come natural to all people. To illustrate this point, introverts bring a level of *trust* that extroverts have to work hard to match. This is not to say extroverts are not trustworthy. An extrovert's enthusiasm sometimes makes them suspect. Extroverts do not need to curb their enthusiasm, but they do need to learn the skills necessary to appear credible. At the same time, extroverts bring a level of *charisma* that introverts have to work hard to match. This does not mean that introverts have to be the life of the party. It does mean they have to learn the skills necessary to appear friendly and enthused about their product. Both personality types can naturally attain *product knowledge* through study and hands-on learning. Whatever your base skill level is, make sure you have the three arrows of selling in your quiver. If you feel you are lacking in these areas, do not worry, as we compare parties to selling you will develop these attributes.

The key to sales success, just like being an excellent party guest, is to be you. Whether you are an introvert or an extrovert, just be yourself and be aware of your personality type. Do not try to be like other salespeople you know. Take your personality and mold it to be a better you. When you are being yourself, you are relaxed and confident and that is powerful when it comes to selling.

That reminds me of a story…

I am by nature an introvert. During my sales career, I found it easy to generate trust among my prospects and my product knowledge was very strong. My client base was very loyal because of these skills. However, there was a hospital I called on where I could never make any progress. Regardless, I kept calling on them. I was persistent. I had been selling for four years and was very successful at what I did. Because of my success, I was promoted to Sales Manager. One of my first acts as a Sales Manager was to hire my brother to sell for our company. My brother is one of the most charismatic people I know. After some training, I decided to let him "cut his teeth" on this hospital I had very little success with. I figured it would be a good experience for him and we had nothing to lose. When we arrived at the hospital the prospect asked my brother why our products are better than the one he currently uses. My brother replied "the product you use is 'goo'". I was stunned by his sophomoric response. I immediately thought I had made a huge mistake hiring my brother. Well, a couple of weeks later I am at the office and I get a phone call from the hospital prospect. The prospect said the following three things to me: "tell your brother that I would like to order twenty of your product; I put a fire extinguisher in my kitchen like he recommended and my wife loved the recipe." At that moment, I learned a very important lesson: A salesperson does not have to sell like me to be successful. My brother had one thing I did not – charisma. He was himself and it resonated with this prospect.

Authenticity, engaging others, and intelligent conversation are the cousins of trust, charisma and product knowledge. These are excellent personal skills at party and excellent business skills during a selling opportunity.

Be yourself and you will be successful.

This week many people need to purchase what you are selling. There is a problem though, you are biased and your prospects know it. You are your worst enemy when you only talk about your product, without building a relationship first. Most of your competitors are talking about their products too. There is no distinction between you and them when you neglect building a relationship.

Imagine a party where everyone is saying the same thing. At a sales presentation, only talking about product would be equivalent to someone only talking about themselves at a party. You would not stay at that party very long, would you?

So, where is the party? Just like the abundant high school parties of your youth, there are plenty of prospects out there. They are waiting for a salesperson like you to show up. Focus on being trustworthy, charismatic and becoming an expert on your product. Most of all – be yourself.

Don't be a Bore

Have you ever been at a restaurant and got one of those waiters who recite the daily specials at your table in the same way they said it at the previous table? It is memorized and canned. (The waiter reminds me of some salespeople.) He might as well be a robot. His presentation does not feel personal and I would rather he not give me his memorized speech and just take my order. His speech is boring! Your customers feel the same way. Seriously, if you get nothing else out of this book – get this: Do not be boring. The definition of boring is someone who only talks about themselves. Boring people are rarely invited to parties. Likewise, boring people rarely make any sales. Do not equate boring with being shy or reserved. Some of the most interesting people I know are laid back and have mastered a wry sense of humor.

How do you avoid being a bore? The key is to know a little about a lot. Read the paper, watch the news, take local and regional road trips, listen to popular music, learn some history, talk to everyone, join a club, read a children's book, surf the net, surf the ocean, enter an adult spelling bee, swing (on a swing set), eat weird foods, litter (kidding). Just be interesting. I could go on forever, but you do not need me to create the list for you. In fact, you do not need a list at all. Just get out there and experience your life and you will have this principle mastered. No one can do this for you.

Salespeople who are boring often rely on objects to strike up interesting conversation. When you visit that prospect for the first time, do not – let me repeat – do not, look around the room at her pictures, awards, gadgets, etc. and then strike up a conversation about something in her office.

What if you did something similar when you first arrived at a party? That would be awkward. At a party, it is best to get to know the host and other guests personally before you talk about items in their home.

Later, as relationships develop you may talk about a piece of art, vase or other items on display. This is the same with your prospect. Become interesting enough that your life and personality can create conversation.

When you know a little about a lot, you will not need to use contrived conversation starters.

While we are talking about unusual, but accepted selling tactics, salespeople should avoid another prevalent and strange practice. The practice of mirroring your prospect's actions, locking eyes with him and repeating his name. This is just plain creepy! Here is a rule of thumb: Say your name when you introduce yourself. Make sure the last word that leaves your mouth as you leave the appointment is the prospect's name. Show him that you remembered his name and let that leave a lasting impact. Say this -"It was a pleasure meeting you – Howard" (or whatever his name really is). Use this same strategy when you talk on the phone.

Contrived conversation starters and mirroring are the tactics of the boring.

Partiers do not do homework, which is why you should not "make a list of interesting things to do". Partiers are living life to its fullest, not making a list. They go where the action is. Remember when your parents said "get out of the house and go play." Your parents were right; you should still "go out and play." This is where you will meet your prospects and add to your life experiences. As your experiences grow, you will begin to have a network of new friends who know people you should connect with. In addition, you will be interesting. It is that simple.

Do not miss the importance of connecting. Someone once said, "Life is more like high school than it is like college. It is who you know, not what you know." Strangely, life is like a popularity contest. For example, most people find new jobs through acquaintances. No reason to fight it, you might as well get on board and start making your own connections.

The best way to build relationships is to be someone who creates connections with other people, for their benefit. The law of connections, and it is a law, is as sure as the law of gravity. This law goes by many names - Reap what you sow, cause and effect, karma, etc. The only catch is that your motivation to connect to others should be pure and authentic. If you do it for selfish gain, you break the law and it will not work.

Right now, you know people looking for jobs, friends, romantic relationships, a house, etc. Figure out whom you can help by connecting them with people you know. It is a very rewarding way to live your life. Do not expect anything in return. The law will take care of that.

How exciting life will be when you seek new experiences, meet new people and help others make important connections. Along the way you will become a more interesting person and be anything but boring. More importantly, you are preparing yourself for significant business relationships.

Before you start telling everyone about your newfound life let us make sure you know another important aspect of selling - how to listen.

Be a Good Listener

We have all met people who dominate conversations and talk only about themselves. They never stop talking long enough to listen to what someone else may have to say.

I sat by a girl on a plane recently and for one hour all she did was talk about herself. Some of it was interesting, but I could have been a wall she was talking too. When a conversation goes one way it is like driving

down a one-way road when the place you want to go is in the other direction. However, I learned a lot about her life by letting her do all the talking.

During business interactions make sure your prospects never feel like a wall. If anybody is going to do a lot of listening, it should be the salesperson.

Even though we just addressed being interesting so you have something to say, you do not want to dominate a conversation. Please understand, you will not be invited to sales presentations if you always talk about yourself. No one wants to hear your sales pitch the first time you meet them. It is contrived and probably not even completely true. It is not that you are dishonest; it is that most sales presentations are heavily weighted in your favor versus being objective. You want to know something else that prospects find annoying? Your elevator pitch. An elevator pitch is that one minute long infomercial, you have practiced 1000 times in the mirror, that you are ready to give someone on an elevator or other short encounter. You might sound as polished as an Oscar winner, but trust me, people are turned off by it.

When a new acquaintance asks "what do you do for a living", what they are really asking is: How have you chosen to spend your time and is it interesting? Just because you sell something that your prospect needs in their business does not mean that they want to meet with you or has any desire to buy from you.

When you meet someone new and they ask the - What you do for a living - question, respond with, "I am a salesperson" and then keep your mouth shut. Do not try to wow them with your fancy, less than honest titles, like account executive or account representative, etc. Be proud that you sell. Everyone sells; you just have the honor of the title. Why should you announce that you are a salesperson and then shut your mouth? The reason is to allow the acquaintance to lead the conversation. I know you were taught as a salesperson to always lead the conversation and take them down certain paths that lead to a sale, but today people are too sophisticated and educated for you to employ this outdated and rude tactic.

Listen to other's stories at a party and ask many questions. Be authentically interested in other's lives. When you listen, you are communicating the respect that everyone desires.

Additionally, keeping your mouth shut prevents you from cramming useless information down your new acquaintance's throat. Let the person ask questions or just talk. If she is talking, you should ask many questions. Be curious and ask the question "why?" a lot. Do not change the subject and talk about yourself or your product. Your only goal at this stage is to be invited to the party, not sell your product. What if this person does not turn out to be a prospect? It is okay because you may have a new friend and if they like you, they may connect you to potential prospects they know.

These conversations are important. If you are talking to someone who buys your products, or who knows someone who buys your products, you may get that coveted invitation to a sales presentation. You are probably thinking that you should do more than just listen. You need to talk about what you sell, right? However, at this point in the relationship do not give a sales pitch; this is the time to tell a story about your new adventurous life and relate it to your career.

To be clear, it is not that you should not talk. Just talk a lot less. Interject stories to get the relationship started.

Tell Stories

People love and respond to stories. It is time to put your heart into your sales presentations and conversations. Intelligence is important, but boring on its own. Use story telling to influence others for the better.

When attending a party you will hear some of the best stories. There is always that person with a crowd around him, laughing and having a good ol' time.

Laughter is the best medicine. I will never forget a sales call I was on at a school district years ago. Another salesperson was already in the prospect's office when I arrived. This salesperson was not a competitor of mine, so the prospect allowed me to sit in the room during the presentation. The prospect said to the salesperson that he would like to place an order for one of the fasteners. The salesperson then took out his order pad and as he wrote said "That will be one *gross*". (A gross is 144 or a dozen, dozen; for the mathematically challenged). At that point, the prospect began to laugh and the

salesperson got a little smirk on his face. I had just witnessed a transition in the sales call and a loosening up of the prospect. I then noticed that the tone of the sales call became relational and conducive to doing business. It is important to note that the salesperson was not trying to scam the prospect. He was being funny, while at the same time he communicated, in an indirect way, that he makes his living from sales and that volume matters. Their meeting concluded on a very successful note and it was clear that they would be doing future business. From that day forward, I have always used humor to say indirectly the things that are hard to say directly and I have tried to inject humor and laughter into every sales call. Life is short; you may as well enjoy it.

When concepts are communicated in story style, you engage the listener and hold their attention until the end of the story. This is more effective than reading bullet points off a slide presentation. Here is an obvious fact about slide presentations – your prospects could read the slides themselves. They do not even need you there. Now, back to storytelling. Story telling is one of the most effective ways to get a point across and can be started with the simple phrase, "That reminds me of a story."

The phrase "That reminds me of a story" comes off the lips and enters the ears of prospects as sweet honey drizzled on white bread. While other salespeople may try to push something on the prospect, you can slow down, keep the atmosphere relaxed and get to know your prospect. Storytelling may seem like a hard thing to do, but actually, it is easy.

Most stories told at a party are not contrived or planned, so do not figure out good stories in advance. You will be so interesting from going out and experiencing life, that stories will just come to you.

This way, when you recount the story, you will be authentic and interesting.

Now, you need some stories to tell.

You can buy books on storytelling that are good, however, listening to others tell stories, noting their enthusiasm and their ability to relive the moment is the best instruction you can get. Real life examples are always best. Hang around storytellers and pay close attention not only to the story, but also to the structure and development of the story.

When telling stories, delivery is important. You sharpen your skills by observing those who already tell stories well. Here are some suggestions - go to a cowboy poetry event, comedy club, read Uncle Remus, volunteer to read at kids story hour. Storytelling is a learn-by-listening art. Do not attempt this on the internet. Get out of the house and go play. Everyone loves stories. Keeping your mouth shut and telling a story go hand in hand. I know that sounds contradictory. The key is timing and if you are going to open your mouth, make sure it is effective.

Like so many areas of life, start small. Start telling stories to family and friends until you feel comfortable. Become known as a storyteller. Change how you tell your stories to see if you get a different response. Do not add to your story and make it untrue. Figure out what to include and omit, emphasize different aspects of the story and figure out the best ending. Human beings naturally tell stories, so you will naturally get better at storytelling as you practice.

Become a person known for telling interesting stories. When you do, you can begin to communicate in a completely new way. Instead of talking about the features of your product, you can tell a story about your product that resonates to the heart of your prospect.

Back in the day, kids use to say "Party Hearty". By this, they meant to party hard and put your heart into it. Human beings need to celebrate and come together with other humans. It is a chance to let your guard down and enjoy life for a short time.

Summary

You are well on your way to a new exciting life as a well-rounded salesperson. Be trustworthy, have charisma and know your product like no other. Once you have these character issues in place, go out and experience life to its fullest. Do not be a bore. As you become this dynamic person, make sure you listen and focus your energy on others. Connecting with other people is one of the secrets to happiness and joy. Find ways to connect others to those who are in need of help. Go out of your way to make connections, even when you are not asked to. Finally, tell stories. Storytelling trumps email, phone calls and even letter writing. The opportunities to sell your product are out there, so make sure you are prepared and understand these concepts.

Once you grasp these concepts, you will be well on your way to the best party ever – your life! Where is the party? It is wherever you are.

Action Points

➤ **Don't be a Bore**

➤ **Be a Good Listener**

➤ **Tell Stories**

Notes:

Chapter Two

Party Planning

When the party invitation comes, you have to prepare to attend. It is the same when you land that appointment with your prospect. What kind of presentation will it be? Will it be a short or long meeting? Will you be presenting to one person or a group of people? You get the picture. Once you know, you can prepare. This is a "know your audience moment." The best entertainers understand the concept of "know your audience." For instance, you do not want to tell inappropriate jokes at a religious convention and you do not want to sing Sinatra songs to fourteen year olds.

Recently I shared a cab ride with two other professional, well-dressed, business people. The cab driver played loud rap music the entire ride making conversation impossible. This is not a comment on rap music; it is a comment on knowing your audience. Another type of music played at a low volume would have been much more appropriate. It would have allowed the business people to talk to each other. I am sure that if the cab driver had catered to his audience his tips would have reflected the extra effort.

Picture the meeting in your mind, just as you do at a party. What will you wear, who will be there and what will be necessary to prepare are all-important considerations. In summary, what would be appropriate?

Appropriateness is a concept that does not get enough attention. As parents, we teach our children appropriateness. For example, we teach them that it is not okay to be loud and silly in a car, however it is just fine to be loud and silly on a playground. As salespeople, we need to be very conscious about appropriateness as well. If you dress well, know who your prospect is and make sure you are on time, you are well on your way to planning appropriately for the sales call.

Dress Well

Party planning starts with what you should wear. C'mon, every day starts with what you should wear.

How you dress is an important part of who you are and communicates an image, good or bad.

In business, you need to know how to dress for a meeting. I believe strongly in this aspect of selling, therefore please understand the emphasis I put on it. Fashion is not only about style, it is about who you are.

Halloween parties and other costume parties say a lot about who you are and the risks you are willing to take. Last year, for Halloween, I dressed up as a CIA Agent. Why? I am in the security business (not the CIA) and I thought it might generate interesting conversation.

Think of yourself as a blank canvas each morning and then paint the picture you want to present (figuratively of course). How you dress for a first appointment matters, just like how you dress for a party matters. This was easy years ago when business suits for men and suited skirts for women were the attire of choice, but today the lines are blurred. The right clothes will make you feel confident and confidence sells. Trust me on this one. What you wear does matter.

I learned this first hand at a business expo. When I first arrived at the expo, someone in a booth put a Hawaiian lei around my neck. I soon forgot I was even wearing it. As I went from booth to booth, I noticed that everyone was talking and joking around with me. It was very different from my normal experience at these expos. Usually, people are somewhat timid and try to read you before they talk to you. I soon realized that people assumed I was fun and easy going based on the fact I was wearing a lei at an expo. The lei around my neck changed the entire dynamic of the expo for me, in a positive way. You can test this

yourself. Try dressing differently than you normally do and watch how many people notice and make comments. Of course, the goal here is not to startle your prospects with outlandish attire, but rather to dress appropriately for what you want to accomplish.

Try to stand out from your competition when it comes to dressing with style. There is a good chance that everyone in your industry dresses the same. Start with the norm and tweak it one notch. If everyone wears suits and ties, dress down a notch by not wearing a tie. If everyone wears khaki's and polo shirts, try dressing up a notch by wearing dress jeans, a long sleeve shirt and a sport coat. A simple way to be noticed positively is to wear cufflinks. For women, this may mean wearing a stylish jacket, chunky necklace or carrying a nice purse with some color. Experiment with different styles at the office or around friends, not in front of prospects. Note the positive or negative reactions and make adjustments accordingly.

Think about parties you have attended. People always notice when someone is dressed nicely or uniquely and they make comments about them.

Your prospect does notice how you dress and it does matter. You are better off dressing lousy than dressing mediocre. Mediocrity is for followers who do everything the same. At least if you dress lousy the prospect might feel sorry for you and make a purchase from you so you can buy your next loaf of bread ☺.

Life is a party – dress up!

Business should be a party – dress up!

Here are three simple tips: *dress your age*, *dress your size* and *dress classy*. In addition, get some help. Have someone with a little fashion sense shop with you and dress you.

Here is another fashion suggestion: Never let the sentence "I dress for comfort" leave your lips. Seek comfort from friends, not clothes. Those words are the mantra of the frumpy. Practice fashion. Dress up to grocery shop, return movies and drop your kids off at school. You never know, you might meet a prospect while doing daily errands.

Dress your age, dress your size and dress classy.

When noticing a man, the first place most people look is at his shoes and wristwatch. Buy the nicest shoes and wristwatch your budget will allow. Keep your shoes shined and use shoetrees – the cedar inserts that keep shoes looking and smelling nice. The wristwatch will help you to be on time to all your appointments. As a woman, try to have a polished, classy look with an up-to-date hairstyle and accessories. Buy clothes that fit correctly and do not draw too much attention to your body.

How you present yourself to your prospect can make the difference between an unsuccessful and a successful sale call.

Man or woman, you can always wear a smile. It is impossible to be unhappy or negative when you are smiling. A smile is a reflection of your attitude and confidence. When you smile, you create a positive first impression, which sets the tone for the rest of the sales call. Additionally, when you set the tone you have more control and a better chance of leading the prospect to a sale. Make sure you practice smiling until it becomes second nature.

Finally, new clothes are an investment in your career. Do not consider them an expense.

Check the Guest List

Wardrobe in place, the next step is to find out who else will be at the party. Will you run into some old friends there or is this a party where you will rub shoulders with the social elite or important executives?

You have to make an impression – right? First, let's discuss your competitors. If you can pull it off, you want to make your sales presentation last. You may glean valuable information while you are waiting your turn. By presenting last, it is common for your prospect to divulge information that was discussed with your competitors, giving you the advantage.

Should you prepare to battle with your competitors prior to showing up? Simply put, you should not prepare to battle them. Your preparation should focus on emphasizing your strengths, not your competitor's weaknesses. Do not "trash talk" your competitors. Instead, talk about your prospect's needs and how you can meet those needs. Your competitors are their own worst enemy, so why even validate them with conversation. If you want to get into public office, stand for something. If you want to make a sale, stand for something. When you are against something, you turn people off.

Often parties have that person who tells secrets, talks badly about others and gossips. While some may seem interested in this pathetic display, ultimately these people are alone, because they cannot be trusted.

How should you prepare for your presentation? Do not forget, you were invited to this party, you are not crashing it, so you need to prepare. You probably know more about your prospect than you think.

Consider what all of your prospects have in common. For example, most prospects are trying to get the best value for their company's money and most prospects are striving for recognition, promotion and advancement.

Once you understand your prospect's common needs, you can prepare presentations that address their needs. This strategy works because most people are similar.

Do not over-think the presentation. Keep it real and do not surf the web to learn every little detail about your prospect's company. When you rattle off facts and figures, you lose authenticity. It is better to know about his industry than it is to know about his company.

Selling is a people business, so make sure you know about key people in their business. Talk about people as much as you can. Search industry associations and peruse their board of directors and prominent leaders. Do not be an encyclopedia. Instead, focus on the people.

You were invited to this party, you are not crashing it.

When you have researched the industry and the people in it, you can talk to your prospect about things they talk about when you are not around. They most likely enjoy discussing the big picture of their industry, more than the details. Win their trust through industry knowledge before you drill down to the details about their company. Find out what industry changes are taking place, who the key people are and what the next big thing is. With this information you will be able to carry on conversations for hours. Make sure you really understand their business world. You do not want to have talking points; you want to have a real grasp on the industry.

When you know who your prospect is, who he works with and what interests him, you are well on your way to a successful presentation and sales call.

However, your progress can be ruined by being late. Always be on time!

Be On Time

You have the classy clothes, a trustworthy wristwatch and you know who is going to be at the meeting. Now, make sure you get directions. Take a little extra time and make sure you know how to get where you are going. There are tools you can use to get directions, so there are really no excuses for getting lost. Be on top of everything you can control like good directions, enough gas, regular maintenance, avoiding speeding tickets, road construction and adjusting for poor weather.

The most overlooked factor that you have control over, but few think about, is parking. Nothing has caused salespeople to be late to more appointments than not scoping out the parking situation. If you think parking will be an issue, it would be advisable to do a dry run at the same time of day as your appointment, exactly one week earlier. You cannot control traffic jams and accidents. Even so, there are internet sites and navigation devices that can help with this too. Have a plan and a back up plan.

Being on time is very important. Whether it is picking up your kids from the babysitter, getting your hair cut or a yoga class – practice being on time. Make this a daily habit.

What does "on time" mean? If you are going to a party that starts at two o'clock, be there at two o'clock. Therefore, you may ask, "what about making an entrance"? By being late? Are you kidding? There are better ways to make an entrance. Have you ever noticed that children's birthday parties always start on time? Being on time is a matter of respect. No one wants to make little Billy or Sally cry on their birthday.

What if you are honestly running late? You have two options. If you are going to be less than ten minutes late, call and let the prospect know that you are running a little late and tell her exactly why you are running late. Do not lie – why would you? It is a sales call after all, not dinner at the White House. What if you are going to be later than ten minutes? Call, apologize and say you would like to postpone the appointment because you do not want to take advantage of her time. Next, ask to reschedule. Then be quiet. She gets to decide what happens next. You will probably get to see her that day. What if she is upset and does not want to reschedule? You probably have lost your opportunity with this prospect. Let us hope this does not happen. The only way to assure that it will not happen is to be on time. Respecting your prospect's time will pay off.

I had lunch with a prospect recently who told me his biggest pet peeve is when salespeople are late and then make up excuses. He said he can deal with the truth and always knows when he is being lied to.

When you see RSVP on a party invitation how much attention do you give this practical formality? A party host has many responsibilities. They are concerned with food preparation, space considerations, seating assignments, etc. When you call in advance, you make their job much easier and give them needed information to make the party better.

When you have a sales appointment, it is not necessary that you call in advance, but doing so surely will make you stand out from the competition. As a courtesy, try calling two business days before the appointment and confirm the location and time. You may be surprised how small acts of respect pay off with big sales.

Summary

We are making real progress. You are defining who you are as a person and a sales person.

How you prepare for sales calls is very important to your success and developing relationships with your prospects.

Dress well and consider what influence you can have by what you wear. Your attire will change how you feel about yourself and how you portray yourself in front of your prospect.

Know your prospect's industry and the people in it. All business is about people, regardless of the product. Get to know your competition so you can better emphasize your strengths, not their weaknesses. Consider the big picture more than the details.

Most importantly, nothing shows respect like being on time.

Party Planning

Action Points

➢ **Dress Well**

➢ **Check the Guest List**

➢ **Be on Time**

Notes:

Chapter Three

Make an Entrance

Okay, now you are getting somewhere. You have figured out who is throwing the party and you have prepared yourself to attend. You have to make a spectacular entrance. An entrance that is memorable. First impressions matter in business just like at parties.

Your demeanor and believing in yourself are important at this stage in the sales process. Love life and love people. When you live a great life, you cannot help but make entrances everywhere you go.

Consider the entrance a bride makes at her wedding. You can learn a lot about selling at a wedding. In reality, a wedding is just a party preceded by a ceremony. The bride has spent a lot of time (her whole life) preparing for the one moment in time when she walks down the aisle. The bride knows that the one thing everyone will remember - is her walking down the aisle.

You too will have put in enormous amounts of time preparing for your first meeting with your prospect. Give as much attention to your first meeting with your prospect as a bride gives to her wedding day. Your entrance will set the tone for the entire relationship.

Love life and love people. When you live a great life, you cannot help but make great entrances everywhere you go.

Make an Entrance

Notice the entrance people make at parties. Most are uneventful which is similar to your competition. However, there are those few that demand the attention of everyone present. Notice the entrances people make at other public places. Some companies use shock marketing to make a huge product splash. Shock marketing is when company executives do crazy stunts to gain attention. The classic stunt is dropping coupons out of a low flying plane into a crowd of people. I am not suggesting you do something outlandish, but do not be like everyone else either. Know your audience and make your decisions based on your audience.

In this chapter, we will discuss the basis for a noteworthy entrance. The areas are confidence, friendliness and a shining personality.

Walk With Confidence

Nothing makes more of an impact than how you walk. Work on your posture. Balance books on your head, if you have to. Fall in love with yourself, because it really helps with confidence. You cannot truly respect others unless you respect yourself. When you feel good about yourself, it seeps out into your physical actions.

Your prospect notices your walk before they listen to your talk.

Some weird chemistry stuff happens when you are confident. Your prospect will sense your confidence and react positively to it.

Once you are at your prospect's site, say hello to everyone. Do this in everyday life too. Make it a part of who you are. If someone asks you how you are doing, do not say, "Good – how are you?" It is rude not to acknowledge his kind comment before returning the question. Instead, respond with, "I am well – *thank you for asking* – how are you?"

If you have to sit in your prospect's waiting area, do not sweat out the appointment. This is a party and you are there to have fun. You are such a well-rounded person that you naturally have a story to tell someone in the lobby, so have a conversation, relax and savor the occasion.

I have found the reception area to be a key place to spend some time and make an impression. The receptionist interacts with everyone in the company and typically has more relationships than anyone else in the company has. Receptionists are often overlooked, when it comes to importance, by both their own colleagues and salespeople. They are the gatekeeper for the company. Many times, they have the discretion to decide which salespeople get in and which do not. Be nice and treat them with extra respect. As their confidence builds in you, you get the added benefit of gaining their respect. If rapport is gained through your interaction with the receptionist, go the extra mile and send her a thank you note, commenting on her kindness.

I observed a sales person trying to gain entrance into a prospect's office. The receptionist called back to the prospect and he answered on the speakerphone. The receptionist asked if he would see the salesperson. The prospect said, "If he has a six-pack of beer, I will talk with him."

Everyone laughed. The salesperson immediately left, bought a six-pack and returned with the beer. Needless to say, he made the presentation and made a sale that day. That is an entrance!

As you make a point of experiencing more of life and stepping outside your comfort zones, your confidence will increase. Your newfound life will dictate your confidence. Confident people are noticed and perceived as authentic. You ooze pride in yourself, your company and your product. Make sure you believe what you are selling. Your beliefs will translate into positive body language.

Confident people are noticed and perceived as authentic.

Be Friendly

After you meet your prospect for the first time, tell her a story about someone you met in the lobby. She needs to know that you are happy to be there and that you are a pleasant person to work with. You are in sales because you love people, right? Okay, money and satisfaction may factor in, but as always, people matter most.

There is no better reason to be in sales than your love of people. You have the best job in the world. Your job consists of visiting old friends and making new ones. Being able to call yourself a salesperson is a gift from above. To be a salesperson means that you can love people twenty-four hours a day and build relationships. Do not even think about striking a balance between your work life and personal life - Integrate them. Good salespeople are all about people, whether it is family, friends, prospects or clients. Enjoy it.

When it comes to friendliness do not change how you are, change who you are. Here is the trick to this change: Smile. Yep, smile. Remember, we already discussed how important this in the *what to wear* section. It is so important it needs to be said again. Smile all the time. Smile when you wake up, smile all day long and finally go to bed with a smile on your face. It is nearly impossible to be unfriendly with a smile on your face. Smile. Smile. Smile.

Every morning when you get dressed, put on a smile.

Friendliness is such a powerful tool that I am amazed how many salespeople are less than congenial. Friendliness is driven by attitude. I like to set goals when it comes to friends. Here are two goals you might consider:

1. Meet one new person each day.
2. Give someone a gift each day.

Meeting new people is easier than you think because most people are lonelier than they are willing to admit. Most people would love to have more friends. There is no such thing as too many friends. The more the merrier. Like any new thing, practice this on a small level. Think of places you frequent and people you see at these places, but do not formally know. Approach them and say, "Hi, my name is (insert your name); I see you here all the time and have wanted to meet you". Try it and you will learn first hand how easy this is. Secondly, give someone a gift each day for no reason at all. The best gifts are given for no reason at all. Be creative and do not worry about the value. It is true, that it is the thought that counts. Find simple ways to give gifts.

I never pass a lemonade stand without making a purchase and then I tip big. To the kids who had the drive to attempt this venture, every sale is like a gift. In addition, when you buy twenty-five cent lemonade for five dollars, trust me, to them it is as good as Christmas. I see it in their faces every time.

An interesting side note: The kids always accept the big tip. We could all learn a lesson here. Be as gracious about receiving gifts as you are about giving them. Do not say, "I couldn't possibly accept this". When you make statements like that, you take all the joy away from the giver. Allow them the pleasure of giving.

I am not saying that you have to be friends with your prospects. However, your prospects are going to respond positively to people who are friendly. Friendly people are magnets that attract other people and opportunities to themselves.

Shine

You are in your prospect's office and now you have to shine. This is your one chance. How do you naturally and effortlessly strike up a relationship with this new friend? You have a wealth of life experiences. You have been expanding your life and knowledge by experiencing new things. Allow this newfound life to burst out of you like sunshine. Have a positive attitude and help others every day. A selfless life is a vibrant life. In addition, take time for yourself. Each day spend some quiet time, exercise and enjoy a harmless vice like occasional coffee breaks.

Personality is an interesting subject. Today being a person has become synonymous with being human. Actually, they are two different things. Humanity is everything our "species" has in common. Personality is everything that makes us unique. This uniqueness is good as long as you are being the true you. Only people can be persons. Further, your personality is a compilation of characteristics you have embraced from others around you. We model what we admire and respect. Understand that being yourself, based on the best attributes of everyone you know, <u>is</u> the best you. Knowing this will go a long way in becoming an ultra successful salesperson.

Think back on some parties you have attended recently. Typically, the memorable people are those with a lot of personality, i.e. uniqueness. This could be the loud person or the quiet person. Both are being uniquely themselves and it is very effective. Conversely, the people who are not being authentic are easily forgotten or ignored as insincere.

Let your quirks out and others will embrace you. You put them at ease to expose their own quirks. This makes interactions comfortable and more conducive to developing long-term relationships. Learn to love other people's quirks. How boring it would be if we were all the same.

Summary

Be confident, friendly and be yourself. Let your shining personality stream out and make an entrance into a new business relationship that will edify your life and your prospect's life.

Action Points

➢ **Walk with Confidence**

➢ **Be Friendly**

➢ **Shine**

Notes:

Chapter Four
Join the Conversation

You have finally arrived at the sales call and made your entrance. Now what? You need to figure out what your prospect has been talking about and join the conversation.

Imagine being at a party and walking up to two people in the middle of a conversation. If you have any manners at all, you would never interrupt and change the topic. What you would do is join the conversation.

Since you know a little about a lot from all of your life experiences, this will be easy for you. Salespeople make a common mistake: They

determine what they think their prospect needs. Why do salespeople do this? They think they know better than the prospect.
Salespeople believe they are an expert in their field because of the time they dedicate to it and the focus they have on their product.
Therefore, salespeople believe their recommendations are as good as gold. You may actually be the expert in your field, but this is no way to carry on a conversation. Talking about what you think is best is similar to interrupting a conversation.

One of the easiest ways to develop a business relationship is to figure out what your prospect is talking about, as it relates to your industry, and talk about the same things. As discussed in an earlier chapter, people who carry on one-sided conversations appear conceited and are rarely invited to form lasting relationships. At your first meeting, join the conversation. Let the prospect lead the conversation and ask many questions.

There will be plenty of time later to educate and close your prospect. This is not the time to close the sale. You need to develop the relationship first. Many salespeople employ the strategy of figuring out their prospects "pain" – what it is that causes their company problems - and then suggest a remedy for the pain. This, of course, is always the salesperson's product. This is a negative approach and should not be implemented until the relationship is solid. It can take months or even years to have a solid relationship with your prospects.

Joining the conversation accomplishes the same thing as discovering their pain, but accomplishes it in a positive way. When you join a conversation, the prospect opens up to you in a way that you can figure out his pain, without focusing on it.

Consider how inappropriate interrupting a conversation at a party would be. Yes, the two in conversation will probably be polite and talk about whatever the person interrupting brings up, but inside they are thinking, "That was rude".

Join your prospect's conversation and develop solutions based on those conversations.

Work the Room

You have developed a solid relationship with your prospect through tried and true manners, ethics and politeness. Now is the time to be bold and stir it up a little bit. This is no different from what you would do at a party. What I am going to recommend is that you ask your prospect for some help. When you ask people for help, they usually will want to help, because it is human nature to want to help. Rarely do you ask someone for directions and they just flat out say "no". Most want to help, if they can. You are going to ask your prospect to make some introductions for you. This is similar to working the room at a party.

At a party, you might ask the host or other key persons to make some introductions for you.

Tell your prospect you would like to meet some other people at her company and other contacts she has in the industry. It does not really matter whom at this point. Set the precedent that you are planning to get to know many people at her company and in her industry. Do not assume you know who the decision makers are. At Disney World, maintenance workers have decision-making power. In addition, "Can I meet the CEO?" is contrived and similar to your competition's approach. When you ask to meet her acquaintances, what you are actually doing is asking for referrals in a polite and professional way. So, whom do you meet? I have no idea. You will figure that out as you get to know your prospect.

The point is not to go to the party and just talk to one person. How boring is that?

Be so different – in a good way – that she will want you to meet her associates. The more people you meet the more entrenched you become in this company. No matter what you sell, you are in the people business. Make many friends. As you meet new people be ultra inquisitive and employ all the techniques that have helped you build a relationship with your prospect. Tap into the narcissism most people possess. Give them a safe outlet to talk. Moreover, tell stories until someone lights a campfire in the lobby and starts making s'mores.

There is a classic sales concept that every sales person should know. It is the rule of seven. As it relates to relationship selling, you should know seven people at every company. When you have that many relationships, you are entrenched and become the incumbent at that company. It is very difficult for your competitors when you are the incumbent. Join the associations your prospect belongs to, attend events with him and get to know the people he knows. When you get to know people and they like you, they automatically introduce you to their friends. Be focused on networking opportunities. Today, we call this viral selling. You infect everyone you come across through your authentic approach to selling.

Too many salespeople "eat and run". Do not be one of these types of salespeople. Be the salesperson who takes his coat off and stays for while. Meet many people and watch your success grow exponentially.

Win Their Trust

You are a salesperson. Salespeople are inherently perceived as untrustworthy. You know you are trustworthy, but your prospect does not. When you win a prospects trust, you are doing your small part to change that perception.

How do you win someone's trust? Start by always telling the truth. Admit that you are biased about your product. Tell your prospect how you believe in your company, but you have a mind of your own.

What should you do if your boss will not allow you to be brutally honest? Then you should start looking for a new job. It is very difficult to sell in a less than honest environment. Moreover, apart from your company's reputation you also have your own reputation to consider. Do not associate with dishonest people or companies. If your reputation is tainted in your territory, it is almost impossible to rebuild.

Be yourself. It is a genius concept that we have discussed in previous chapters. If you have quirks, do not hide them – be real. Nothing sells like honesty, authenticity and being you. A common trait of excellent sales people is that they are brutally honest. Prospects need to trust you and feel that you are being authentic. Many prospects wish they could trust their salespeople. This opens up opportunities for you to stand out – based on honesty. How nice would it be if every sales call were sincere and authentic?

At a party, you can always tell those guests that exaggerate and embellish stories and events.

The only thing worse than exaggeration and embellishment is being vindictive or gossiping. Usually gossipers are left off future guest lists.

Ultimately, vindictive people and gossipers are trying to impress, but it is a false attempt at popularity and this "lying" is usually rejected by others. However, it adds excitement to a story when you are theatrical. Do not hesitate to emphasize important points or characters in your story with voice inflections and body movements.

In selling, do not badmouth your competitors in an effort to win a sale. Talk about what you do well, answer questions honestly and the sales will naturally follow. As we discussed in an earlier chapter, trust, charisma and product knowledge are the trinity when it comes to successful selling. Trust establishes stable and secure relationships.

Nothing sells like honesty.

Shakespeare said, "To thine own self be true". In essence, stop lying to yourself. Be honest in every aspect of your life. Nothing will build your reputation like honesty. I am not lying about the importance of honesty. Once you have earned the prospects trust you are well on your way to a long term, successful relationship.

Don't try too Hard

People buy from people. People take care of people. A company cannot do a thing to help your prospect. How many times does a salesperson say, "Let me tell you about my company"? Change that to let me tell you about Steve or Karen or Tammy. People solve problems. When you receive phone calls or emails asking how your company can fix a certain problem, tell them about a particular person, brag about their knowledge and explain how they solved a similar problem for (insert prospects name) at (*XYZ*) company. You are communicating a personal solution to a business problem. Your prospects will find this refreshing. It is people helping people, not companies helping companies and that gets positive responses from prospects.

To keep things in perspective, remember you work for your boss, not a company. A company is merely an entity employing real people. Your satisfaction is closely tied to your relationship with your boss. However, strong companies are important to your success. They provide the financial resources that allow people to help people. They are essential and should be revered. Without a strong company behind you, the people in your organization could not perform the way they do. Be sure to keep a proper perspective between your company and your support staff.

It is time to discuss the actual presentation you will make to your prospect.

First, what *not* to do in a presentation. As mentioned earlier, please do not use slide presentation software. Seriously, it is so boring and archaic. Your prospect can read the slide faster than you can read it to them. You could email the slides and they could read them without you there. It would be better to draw little pictures and hand them to your prospect than to bore him with a slide presentation. If you are dead set on using slide software, I would recommend you buy a few books on how to do this type of presentation properly. Remember, you want to make a memorable presentation, not a boring one.

What should you do? Be relaxed and conversational. Ask questions to determine what interests him. Then, tell a story that demonstrates how your product is the solution for your prospect's needs. Yes, use stories to make your points. Treat this as you would any personal relationship.

Once you decide on how you are going to represent yourself and your company, be sure not to try too hard. Good presentations are interactive and communicative. You are making a new friend. Your prospect can tell when you are desperate and he knows that desperados are uninspiring people to work with.

Parties with agendas seem to carry a level of stress associated with them. They are not as enjoyable and relaxing as parties that are simply a "get together".

It may be one of the oldest clichés ever, but *"go with the flow"* is the best way to develop long-term relationships. In other words, be at ease during your sales call and don't try to hard.

At parties, you will run into many unexpected situations. Once I went to a party that was highly attended by people I differ with politically. If I had tried too hard to make my point, it would have been a miserable time for all. It is possible to have strong beliefs and still get along with those whom you differ. The need to make your point is a sign of insecurity on your part, which translates into desperation.

Do not act desperate. Have some fun. There are not any good reasons to be desperate because there are always more prospects, just like there are always more parties to go to.

A word of warning: Be loose, but be careful about telling jokes. Really, you are not as funny as you think you are. What can be effective is to make fun of yourself, followed by a laugh. If you are going to make light of yourself make sure you really mean it. If you are a nerd, say so. If you are clumsy, say so. Let them know the real you.

Summary

There is no magic to a good sales presentation. Use your manners and join the conversation. Tell stories to illustrate your points. Talk about what interests your prospect

and selling opportunities will present
themselves.

Join the Conversation

Action Points

➢ **Work the Room**

➢ **Win Their Trust**

➢ **Don't try too Hard**

Notes:

Chapter 5

Clean Up or Leave

You should feel proud. You were invited to the party, prepared well and you were polite. At the sales meeting, you focused on the prospect and listened to their needs. You told stories and related how your people can meet the prospect's needs. You have demonstrated the three key elements of good salesmanship: trust, charisma and product knowledge. Now, the party is ending and you need to clean up or leave. In other words, how do you close?

I think salespeople try to do too much too fast. Let the relationship develop before you try to close a sale.

At a party, you would not finish the night with get-to-know you questions. Early in the party, you ask questions and get to know people, not at the end.

Closing can be the easiest part of the sale when you allow things to develop. The right time to ask for their business becomes obvious. The days of pressuring people into sales are long gone. Prospects know when they are being sold and become defensive. How do you graciously and effectively end your sales call? Ponder that question, because it is crucial to your success.

In this chapter, we will address three closes. Grasping these concepts and adapting them to your specific business will improve your sales results.

Leaving is the Best Close

It is better to leave the appointment than to fumble through a contrived or planned close. Many times, you may not want or need to close the sale. Stay focused on building the relationship and let the close come to you. Your prospects will communicate when it is the right time to close. This is why listening is so important. Allow your prospects to make decisions based on your relationship instead of asking them to buy your product.

Forget all the cliché closes you have been taught. Here is a crazy thought: Sometimes leaving is the best close of all.

When you are at a party and the host starts signaling the party is ending – and there are signals - you should graciously prepare to leave. How you leave may determine if you are invited to the next party.

Focus on creating life-long relationships and you will have plenty of chances to close the sale at a later date. When you leave at the right time, you are gaining a level of respect that is tough to come by any other way.

The Gracious Close

As you are leaving say something like, "I had a wonderful time getting to know you. We should do this again." Similar to what you would say when leaving a party. Then finish by stating his name – "It was a pleasure to meet you (Mr. Prospect)." That is how you leave a party and that is how you leave a sales appointment. I call this *the gracious close*.

When you use the gracious close, you are using manners that have long been forgotten in today's modern world. Read some books on personal and business etiquette. It is amazing how people respond to common courtesies. Most of the time they do not even realize why they are responding so positively. These common courtesies work because they always show respect and communicate that the other person is more important than you.

Do not Leave Anything Behind

How often do salespeople give a mediocre presentation and call it good because they know they are going to leave a professionally written sales brochure behind. Salespeople think the brochure somehow makes up for their inadequacies. This happens a lot. Do not leave something behind. Do not lean on that crutch.

Who came up with the marketing idea of the sales brochure? There is nothing wrong with the concept, but it has become the substitute for selling.

If you were leaving a party and handed out a flyer about how wonderful you are and why you should be invited back by the host, think how weird that would be. I hope that early at the party you told a few stories, joined a few conversations and piqued enough interest that the guest asked all the questions that the flyer would have addressed.

You may not know it, but you have been selling and closing all along. That is, you have been selling yourself as a very interesting person. After all, the prospect is buying you, not your product. He can find good product anywhere.

Often, when parties are held during the winter months, the host places all the coats on a bed. It seems that someone usually forgets his or her coat or some other item is left behind on the bed. It becomes a hassle for the host to arrange returning the coat.

In the same sense, do not leave your brochure behind. If you are going to leave something behind, leave a favorable memory of you. Sounds corny, but it is very important. When you focus on your relationship with your prospect in a dynamic and authentic way, he cannot help but remember you.

I like to ask permission to email more information as a follow up to our meeting. This gives you an opportunity to follow up on a promise and following through builds trust.

The Promise Close

Years ago, a Sales Manager taught me to make very specific promises. If I called a prospect on the phone and they were not interested, I would ask permission to call them back three months later. If they agreed, I would then say, "Thank you, I will call on Tuesday, August 8 at exactly 2:37PM." Normally, this would catch their attention, but at that point, they just wanted me off the phone. Then, when August 8 rolled around, I would call them at exactly the time I promised and remind them of my promise.

As you can imagine, this really got their attention and was very effective. I call this the "promise close." Make very specific promises and then follow through.

If You are Going to Stay – Clean Up

The ultimate purpose of being in sales is to make sales. Those with strong relationships and excellent manners are welcomed back by prospects and have a very successful and fulfilling career.

When you attend a party, it is always appropriate to offer to stay and help clean up. If you host parties, you know what how nice this help can be. If the party ends at ten o'clock, you could be up until one in the morning just getting the house in order. It is always nice to have a little help and a chance to have a more intimate conversation than a party allows.

In the above illustration, cleaning up relates to closing the sale. The only reason to stay longer than the presentation allows is to close the sale.

The Offer Close

If you want to attempt a very effective close, ask this question – "What else can I do for you?" I call this the "offer close." You have probably heard this question before. It is a great question that opens up many possibilities. Most prospects will say, "I am good, thank you". The trick is not to stop with the question – continue with something like, "helping others is what I do for a living and I am available 24/7 for you". If you are not available 24/7, you should re-evaluate your career choice. As a salesperson, you have an integrated life. Always working and always partying. Tell your prospects they can call you at two o'clock in the morning, if they need to.

Most prospects will never call you in the middle of the night, but let them know they can if needed. It is the fact that you made a generous offer that matters!

Using the offer close allows your prospect to tell you if he would like to do business with you. It may be as simple as him asking you for specific information, requesting a proposal, or a sample product or even indicating he would like to purchase your product.

Summary

The best words you will ever hear from your prospects are these: "Thank you for coming, please come again." Build lifelong relationships and you will hear this often.

Action Points

> ➤ **Leaving is the Best Close**

> ➤ **Do not Leave Anything Behind**

> ➤ **If You are Going to Stay – Clean Up**

Notes:

Party On!

After the Party

All good parties must end. My hope is that this book seemed like a party. What do you do the day after a party? Send your prospect a thank you note.

Sending a thank you note is a classic demonstration of your professionalism and respect.

If you really want to impress, handwrite a note on personal stationary. Handwritten notes are read and appreciated. Your prospect knows that a hand written note took time and makes them feel important.

Think about your personal and business mail. With all the bills, marketing pieces and junk mail, isn't it nice to receive a hand written note from a friend or colleague?

Structure your note something like this:

Date
Dear (Prospect),

Line One: Tell her how she affected you.

Line Two: Give an example of the affect.

Line Three: Thank her for her professionalism or some other personal characteristic.

(Never thank her for the appointment. Emphasize what about her motivated the appointment.)

Sincerely,
(Your Name)

Party Favors

"Do your work; not just your work and no more, but a little more for the lavishing's sake -- that little more which is worth all the rest."

Dean Briggs

Favorite Books

available at:

www.WardFigge.com

➢ Never Eat Alone: And Other Secrets to
Success, One Relationship at a Time
Keith Ferrazzi

➢ The Richest Man in Babylon
George S. Clason

➢ Secret Service: Hidden Systems That
Deliver Unforgettable Customer Service
John R. DiJulious

➢ How to be Motivated All the Time
Peter J. Daniels

➢ The Etiquette Advantage in Business
Peggy Post, Peter Post

- Verbal Judo: The Gentle Art of Persuasion
  George Thompson

- Business Notes: Writing Personal Notes that Build Business Relationships
  Florence Isaacs

- Setting the Table: The Transforming Power of Hospitality
  Danny Meyer

- Choose the Right Word
  S.I. Hayakawa

- Cod
  Mark Kurlansky

- The Shack
  William P. Young

Be my Facebook Friend

Search:

Ward Figge

You can also be a Fan of this Book

Search:

Selling Uncorked

Recipe for Success

Instead of taking your prospects donuts or bagels, try this: Make a pecan log from scratch and deliver these tasty morsels to your next appointment. Make sure you tell them you made them yourself. There is something about food, made by hand, that connects people at a deeper level.

32 ounces of chopped pecans
1 box of vanilla wafers
2 cans (28oz) of condensed milk

Crush the wafers and mix all the ingredients together in a large bowl. On wax paper, roll mixture into four, one-foot long logs. Refrigerate overnight. Cut log into 1/3" thick slices and deliver to your prospect. Watch the sales start rolling in. ☺

Index

About the Author

For over 15 years, Ward Figge has been creating business cultures where salespeople love their work and excel in selling. He has endeared a loyalty seldom seen in today's business world. In his book, *Selling Uncorked*, Ward Figge uses traditional business concepts, storytelling and analogies to keep his readers engaged. Ward Figge is employed by a major corporation where he applies these principles daily.

www.ingramcontent.com/pod-product-compliance
Lightning Source LLC
Chambersburg PA
CBHW071719170526
45165CB00005B/2074